Collection Management Development Guides, N(

GUIDE FOR WRITING A BIBLIOGRAPHER'S MANUAL

The Collection Management
and Development Committee
Resources and Technical Services Division
American Library Association

Carolyn Bucknall, chair
Subcommittee on Guide for Writing a Bibliographer's Manual

AMERICAN LIBRARY ASSOCIATION

Chicago and London 1987

Composed by Deborah Doering
in Times on an Apple Macintosh Plus™
with a 20 MB Hard Disk using Aldus'
Pagemaker™ Software, version 2.0.

Printed on 60-pound Heritage
Antique Book, a Ph-neutral stock,
and bound in 10-point Carolina cover
stock by Imperial Printing Company
∞

Library of Congress Cataloging-in-Publication Data

Guide for writing a bibliographer's manual.

   (Collection management and development guides; no. 1)
   Includes index.
   1. Collection development (Libraries)—Handbooks, manuals, etc.—
Authorship. 2. Bibliographers—In-service training. 3. Library administration.
4. Libraries—Aims and objectives. I. Bucknall, Carolyn. II. American Library
Association, Collection Management and Development Committee. III. Series.
Z687.G84   1987   025.2'0202   87-17574
ISBN 0-8389-3343-2

Copyright © 1987 by the American Library Association. All rights reserved except those
which may be granted by Sections 107 and 108 of the Copyright Revision Act of 1976.
Printed in the United States of America.

93 92 91 90   5 4 3 2

CONTENTS

Preface

1. Introduction to this guide
1.1. Purpose of this guide
1.2. Need for this guide
1.3. Intended audience and scope of this guide
1.4. Definitions of words and terms as used in this guide

2. Bibliographer's manual: Introduction
2.1. Audience for manual
2.2. Purposes and objectives of manual
2.3. Scope of manual
2.4. Provision for revision

3. The institutional context and its documentation
3.1. The context of the parent institution
3.2. The context of the existing collection development and management program
3.3. The context of the library as a whole
3.4. The external context

4. Administration of the collection development and management program
4.1. Organizational structure of the collection development and management program
4.2. Administrative obligations and responsibilities
4.3. Tools for collection development planning and decision making
4.4. Recruiting bibliographers
4.5. Orientation and training

4.6.	Performance evaluation and goal setting
4.7.	Professional development opportunities
4.8.	Calendar of events
5.	The bibliographer or subject specialist
5.1.	Introduction
5.2.	Intellectual and professional development
5.3.	Job duties or responsibilities

Index

PREFACE

This guide has been widely reviewed by librarians from a variety of libraries. Draft copies were mailed to over one hundred interested librarians before the public hearing held at the American Library Association Midwinter Meeting in Chicago on January 20, 1986, and an additional hundred were distributed at the hearing. The text was extensively revised to incorporate comments by these reviewers.

A difficulty that could not be entirely resolved was terminology. The most appropriate designation for the librarian who engages in collection development and management was the subject of much debate. Does one expect to find a *bibliographer* only in an academic library environment? Might not *collection developer* be a better choice? Or *collection manager*? But the meanings of *collection development* and *collection management* are not themselves uniformly perceived in the library profession. In this matter the committee took *collection development* to be the larger term, subsuming such bibliographer concerns as collection management, liaison with clientele, selection of materials and fund management. A *collection manager* would be involved in less than the full range of possible bibliographer activities. A *selector* would be similarly restricted. And, though the broadest definition for *collection development* was adopted for purposes of this guide, the committee also recognized that the term in many libraries is still synonymous with *selection* alone. *Collection developer* was at length ruled out as carrying a possibly limiting subliminal message. In the end the committee chose *bibliographer*.

Preservation specialists and administrators, some representing the Preservation of Library Materials Section of the Resources and Technical Services Division, also reviewed the guide, and the final text includes many references to preservation issues and concerns. However, the context—guidance for writing a bibliographers' manual—did not permit detailed consideration of preservation as it relates to collection development.

Thanks are extended to early contributors on the committee's work: David Perkins, Richard Ring, Martin Faigel, and Connie McCarthy. Additionally, the helpful suggestions of Lynn Jones and Lorraine Rutherford, Ross Atkinson, Esther Bierbaum, Daniel Callison, and Barbara Lockett were appreciated. Also of assistance were comments from Bonita Bryant, Judi Fouts, Norman Horrocks, Linda Gould, and Margaret Murray. Gratitude is expressed, finally, to those librarians who attended the public hearing and advised on improving the guide.

CAROLYN BUCKNALL

1. Introduction to this guide

1.1. Purpose of this guide

This guide is intended to help librarians write a bibliographer's manual that can serve as an informational, administrative, and training document for their library's collection development and management program.

1.2. Need for this guide

Librarians around the nation in all types of libraries are confronting a series of similar problems and challenges in building, maintaining, and preserving collections. While library economic resources have declined, the production of information has accelerated, and user demands for information in new as well as traditional formats have risen. At the same time problems related to the deterioration of library materials and, frequently, to limited space have further complicated collection management. In response to these pressures libraries variously have altered organizational structures, realigned resources, increased technological support, and developed cooperative arrangements. Each of these actions has in turn embodied new challenges for bibliographers.

Taken together, current issues and challenges have made collection development and management functions more complex. Formal library education for bibliographers typically has focused on only one element of collection development and management: principles of book selection. Attendees at a 1977 RTSD Collection Development Preconference in Detroit expressed a need for education and training that address the broader spectrum of collection development and management functions. Participants at the 1981 RTSD Pilot Regional Collection Management and Development Institute at Stanford University and at subsequent regional institutes explicitly noted the importance and usefulness of a bibliographers' manual, particularly for documenting collection development and management practice in a systematic way.

1.3. Intended audience and scope of this guide

The guide offers librarians writing a bibliographers' manual a wide array of points for possible inclusion in their own manuals. These options are potentially applicable to a range of collection development and management programs in a variety of libraries: public, school, academic, and special. The guide, while identifying possible individual considerations, reminds manual compilers to weigh carefully local needs and objectives in selecting from the more comprehensive lists of options. Manual compilers are encouraged to make common-sense adaptations of this guide.

1.4. Definitions of words and terms as used in this guide

1. *approval plan*—A contractual arrangement by which a bookdealer assumes the responsibility for selecting and supplying, subject to return privileges, all publications, as currently issued, fitting a library's collection profile specified in terms of disciplines, levels of difficulty, languages, countries of origin, formats, etc.
2. *bibliographer*—A library staff member, typically possessing superior knowledge of a discipline, whose responsibilities include aspects of development and management of the library's information resources in the subject field(s) of his or her specialization; also referred to as a selector, subject specialist, or collection developer.
3. *blanket order*—A contractual agreement by which a publisher supplies a library one copy of all publications or media productions, as currently issued, within specified limits, generally without return privileges.
4. *collection development*—The process of planning, building, and maintaining a library's information resources in a cost-efficient and user-relevant manner, its principal activities including the identification, selection (and sometimes procurement) of locally appropriate materials; the allocation of the resources budget among different subjects and formats; collection management, analysis, and evaluation; liaison with library users; planning and implementation of resource sharing and related programs, as well as the determination and coordination of policies and procedures governing these functions.
5. *collection development and management program*—The formal organization of a library's collection development and management activities in a systematic manner, explicitly linked to the parent agency's mission, administratively structured around corresponding goals and objectives, and supported by appropriate policies, governance arrangements, training programs, etc.
6. *collection development officer*—The library staff member responsible for administering the library's collection development and management program.
7. *collection development policy*—A written document defining the scope and nature of a library's existing collections and the policies and plans for continuing development of resources, with precise designation of present collection strengths and current collecting inten-

---

*Definition adapted from *The ALA Glossary of Library and Information Science*, ed. Heartsill Young (Chicago: American Library Association, 1983).

sity in relevant subject fields and a statement of selection philosophy as related to institutional goals, general selection criteria, and intellectual freedom.

8. *collection management*—Activities that are designed to make optimum use of existing information and fiscal resources to assure maximally effective collection development, employing techniques such as vendor and dealer assessments; collection analysis and evaluation; use and user studies; and collection review for preservation, protected access, remote storage, or discard.

9. *conservation*—Treatment of a single object intended to maintain or improve its physical condition.

10. **continuation order*—An order to a dealer or publisher to supply the various parts of a serial or series until otherwise notified.

11. **core list*—A list of works considered essential for the study of a particular discipline, especially a basic list of periodical titles in a subject field.

12. **depository arrangement*—A legal agreement which entitles a library to receive, generally without cost, all or a selected portion of the documents issued by a government (national, state, municipal, etc.) or an international organization.

13. *disaster preparedness plan*—A document that outlines a library's policy and procedures for responding to emergencies which threaten physical resources and that specifies priorities and techniques for salvaging different types of material in the event of their damage by fire, flood, vandalism, or other kinds of disasters.

14. *disposition policy*—A policy that states the options for disposing of materials acquired by purchase, gift, deposit, etc., as governed by local, parent agency, legal, and other considerations. These options include adding to the collection, exchanging, giving to other agencies, sale, and discarding.

15. **exchange agreement*—An arrangement by which a library sends to another library its own publications or productions, or those of other agencies, and receives in return publications or productions from the other library; or sends duplicates from its collection and receives other materials in return.

16. *fund allocation*—The administrative process of distributing the monies available for the acquisition of materials and other information resources among different subject areas, collections, formats etc.

17. *gathering plan*—One of several types of contractual agreements by which a publisher or bookdealer supplies to a library current publications or media productions as they are issued, with specific stipulations as to scope of materials to be included, return privileges, etc. Approval plans and blanket orders are types of gathering plans.

---

*Definition adapted from *The ALA Glossary of Library and Information Science,* ed. Heartsill Young (Chicago: American Library Association, 1983).

18. *media*—Materials in all formats and all channels of communication that serve as carriers of information with the exception of conventional print materials, including non-print materials, computer software, textual and numeric data bases, and similar electronic resources.
19. *preservation*—A broad range of activities intended to retard, stop, or prevent deterioration of materials or to retain the intellectual content of materials no longer physically intact. Preservation includes such collection management activities as the selection of replacement copies, the identification of items for retention in storage or protected access, and the selection of materials for transfer to alternate formats such as microforms.
20. *standing order*—A general order to a dealer or publisher to supply volumes or parts of a particular title or other type of non-serial publication as they appear, until notified otherwise.
21. *subscription*—An arrangement by which, in return for a pre-paid sum, a periodical, newspaper, or other serial is provided for a specified number of issues.

2. Bibliographer's manual: Introduction

The introduction to the manual should define the intended audience, purpose and scope of the manual. Statements of need and definitions of special terms are also appropriate to the introduction.

2.1. Audience for manual

The intended audience for the manual is usually collection development and management practitioners, including collection development and management administrators.

Other target groups may be non-bibliographer supervisors of bibliographers, library directors, other library administrators, other library staff, and administrators or officers of the parent agency.

2.2. Purposes and objectives of manual

The purpose of the manual should be explicitly stated, for example, to bring together essential documentation for carrying out collection development and management activities in a specified library.

Specific objectives that might be sought include the following:
1. to document collection development practice in a systematic way
2. to aid individual bibliographers in carrying out collection development and management responsibilities
3. to assist in the administration of the collection development and management program

*Definition adapted from *The ALA Glossary of Library and Information Science,* ed. Heartsill Young (Chicago: American Library Association, 1983).

4. to provide a training tool for new bibliographers
5. to provide a planning tool for individual bibliographers to measure progress of work or improve its quality
6. to establish and document the basis for performance evaluation of bibliographers
7. to foster better communication between individual bibliographers
8. to inform librarians who are not bibliographers about collection development and management activities
9. to inform non-librarians about collection development and management activities

2.3. Scope of manual

The introduction should include a summary statement regarding the manual's scope. The possible scope of the manual, as outlined in this guide, begins with section 3. However, the scope of individual manuals will vary considerably, depending on individual conditions and needs.

2.4. Provision for revision

Stated plans for revision will emphasize the intended flexibility, timeliness, and utility of the manual. A loose-leaf format, produced on a word processor if possible, permits frequent revision as needed.

3. The institutional context and its documentation

The contents of the manual will be conditioned by the institutional context, including the context provided by the parent institution or agency, the existing collection development and management program, the library as a whole, and external factors. The following aspects of institutional context should be considered for appropriate documentation and inclusion.

3.1. The context of the parent institution

Mission and goals statements of the parent institution or agency, the library as a whole, and the collection development and management program of the library should be included in the manual insofar as possible. A section on libraries in a city charter, for example, may contain the parent agency's mission and goals statement for a public library. Goals of the collection development and management program may overlap in some measure with those of other areas of the library.

3.1.1. Agencies having advisory or oversight responsibility for the library: e.g., Board of Trustees, Faculty Library Committee, School Board of Education

3.1.2. Agencies other than the library having similar function within the parent institution

3.2. The context of the existing collection development and management program

3.2.1. General approach to materials selection

The manual describes factors in the existing operational environment that condition selection. Only broad statements of prohibition or permission should be included. The articulation of general concepts such as the extent of purchasing current and retrospective materials, serials and monographs, media, duplicate titles, etc., is most appropriate to the collection development policy and need not be duplicated here, though reference to these concepts may be useful.

3.2.2. Acquisitions strategy

The manual may include a statement on the overall acquisitions strategy. Such a statement would address the mix of methods by which materials are acquired and the degree of dependence on each: gathering plans (blanket orders, approval plans, depository arrangements, memberships), continuing acquisitions (standing orders, subscriptions, continuations), item-by-item purchases, and gifts and exchanges. Considerations determining the strategy employed, such as timely acquisitions, reasonable cost of materials and services, and effective use of available staff in the selection and acquisition process, should be explained.

3.2.3. The collection development policy

Specific approaches to materials selection should be detailed in a separate, written collection development policy. Generally, information contained in the collection development policy need not be repeated in the manual. However, a brief account of the history and present status of the library's collection development policy would be useful.

3.2.4. Other publications and policies

The bibliographer's manual is not intended to replace existing manuals. However, other internal publications and policies affecting the existing collection development and management program will condition the contents of the manual.

The manual should list these other local publications and policies and indicate where they may be found. Examples of possible publications of this type follow:

1. materials selection policy (for public library users)
2. acquisitions manual for faculty and students (for academic library users)
3. copyright guidelines
4. disposition policy
5. gifts policy
6. preservation manual
7. preservation policy
8. disaster preparedness plan

9. guidelines for serials selection and cancellation
10. collection evaluator's manual
11. transfer policy
12. weeding policy
13. offsite storage policy
14. withdrawals and replacements policy
15. policy on depreciation and replacement of hardware

Include also references to documents recounting the history of the collection as it has affected the evolution of collecting priorities.

3.3. The context of the library as a whole: other library functions interacting with the collection development and management program, and the documentation of their procedures

Particularly in small and medium-sized libraries where one individual is responsible for several types of activities, bibliographers may have adequate opportunity to gain detailed knowledge of procedures that affect the collection development and management program. Generally, the larger the library, the greater the necessity for documentation of procedures in other functional areas relevant to the work of bibliographers. As necessary, the manual should include such documentation or references to where the documentation may be found.

3.3.1. The following list identifies functions that, while related to collection development and management, may or may not be organizational components of the program. The list is not exhaustive and includes potential organizational overlap.

1. acquisitions, monographic and serials
2. pre-order searching
3. binding
4. collection maintenance
5. preservation/conservation
6. cataloging
7. circulation
8. interlibrary services
9. facilities
10. fund raising
11. gifts and exchanges
12. public relations
13. government documents
14. online data bases
15. reference

3.3.2. Nature of documentation

The manual may usefully explain the functional relationships between collection development and management and other areas of the library;

flow charts can be helpful in showing how library orders and receipts go through the system. At a minimum the manual and automated files essential to collection development and management activities in the particular library should be identified and defined. List these files together with their location, scope, and purpose.

In summary, use documentation that enables the bibliographer to understand the library context for the collection development and management program; and include information on procedures and files necessary to conduct collection development and management activities.

3.4. The external context

3.4.1. National standards, published guides and guidelines

Professional organizations and other agencies of national scope issue many standards, guides, and guidelines which can be useful in developing a collection development and management program. Many of these publications are directed to particular types of libraries or to specialized library functions, such as preservation.

The manual may include the actual text or refer to publications or issuing bodies with which the bibliographer should be familiar. Libraries are encouraged to make as many locally relevant titles accessible as possible, perhaps by establishing a bibliographers' reference shelf. Examples of issuing agencies and some of their publications follow. Since complete lists of current publications may be obtained from these agencies, only a few specific titles of particular usefulness are mentioned. Publication dates are not cited because typically this type of publication undergoes frequent revision.

1. American Library Association, "Library Bill of Rights"
2. Resources and Technical Services Division, Resources Section: guides, guidelines, price indexes
3. guidelines and accreditation standards issued by the Department of Education or similar agency in the various states
4. Association for Educational Communications and Technology/American Library Association, *Media Programs: District and School*
5. Association for College and Research Libraries: standards and guidelines
6. National Information Standards Organization (formerly Committee Z39 of the American National Standards Institute): standards
7. American National Standards Institute: standards (other than those issued by the National Information Standards Organization)
8. library statistics issued by the U.S. National Center for Educational Statistics, Association of Research Libraries, and other agencies

9. *Selection of Library Materials in the Humanities, Social Sciences, and Sciences,* Patricia A. McClung, editor (Chicago, American Library Association)
10. Library Binding Institute, *Standards*
11. Association of Research Libraries, Preservation Committee, "Standards for Minimum Preservation Efforts"
12. Research Libraries Group, *Preservation Manual*
13. Association of Research Libraries, Office of Management Studies, NCIP materials

3.4.2. Coordinated or cooperative activities

Libraries increasingly have taken active roles in establishing coordinated or cooperative activities that extend their resources beyond their own institution. Include in the manual details of all the library's continuing coordinated and cooperative activities relating to the development and management of information resources:

1. reciprocal loan agreements
2. coordinated collection development through participation in local, regional, or national agreements, networks, or consortia and in committees or boards related to these groups
3. cooperative preservation activities
4. other (examples: National Shelflist Measurement Project, North American Collections Inventory Project, Eighteenth Century Short Title Catalog)

4. Administration of the collection development and management program

This section of the manual is intended to provide the bibliographer with an overview of organizational structure, administrative obligations and responsibilities, tools for planning and decision making, recuiting and training, evaluation and goal setting, professional development, and a general calendar of annual activities for the collection development and management program.

4.1. Organizational structure of the collection development and management program

A statement describing the entire library organization should be the first element in the section on administration, followed by a description of how the collection development and management program is facilitated within that structure. The latter should relate the collection development and management program to its user community (e.g., the general public, faculty and students, the corporate staff) and to other organizational areas of the library. In public school systems library organizational relationships will extend to the school district level and may include a learning resources, media, or library supervisor. These relationships may be conveyed by job descriptions, organization charts and other diagrams, as well as by textual material.

4.1.1. Library organization chart

A chart of the entire library organization can offer a visual representation of the organizational relationships, lateral and vertical, between, for example, the collection development officer, bibliographer coordinators, bibliographers, and support staff, as well as between collection development practitioners and supervisors in other programmatic areas of the library.

4.1.2. Organization chart or other diagram showing the relationships of personnel in the collection development and management program

A detailed diagram of the collection development and management program within the larger organization reveals with more specificity and in more depth the relationships among staff having collection development responsibilities. The diagram may also include less formal governance structures, such as standing committees, that influence and determine program goals.

4.1.3. Directory of collection development and management staff showing subject, area studies, or programmatic assignments.

4.1.4. Support staff

The manual should describe the character and number of support staff for the collection and management program and their appropriate use by the individual bibliographer. Supervisory responsibilities for support staff must be clearly delineated.

4.1.5. Committees and other similar groups

List the local standing committees and other similar groups that influence or determine collection development program decisions, including for each the charge or purpose statement, basis for selection, term of service, and the individual to whom the group reports. Committees established in the larger institutional context may also be mentioned when they require library representation.

Examples of groups to be listed are:
1. Collection Development Committee
2. Preservation Committee
3. Disaster Action Team
4. Bibliographers' Council
5. Media Selection Committee
6. District Committee on Challenges to Materials
7. Curriculum Development Committee

4.2. Administrative obligations and responsibilities

Descriptions of specific obligations and responsibilities relating to the administration of the collection development and management program.

Include here the administrative responsibilities of both the Collection Development Officer and the bibliographer whose work is coordinated by the officer. (These obligations, which are detailed below, are distinct from the bibliographer job reponsibilities mentioned in 4.4.3 and enumerated in 5.3 of these guidelines.)

4.2.1. Collection Development Officer obligations and responsibilities relating to the administration of the collection development and management program

The following responsibilities are examples only and may vary considerably from one library to another; some may be shared with bibliographers:

1. preparing budgets and fund allocation
2. representing the collection development and management program to the library administration
3. representing need for adequate support for bibliographers (e.g., for typing, computer input, searching) and, in the case of a bibliographer assignment for someone already on the staff, negotiating sufficient time to perform expected duties
4. recruiting and training bibliographers
5. maintaining communication with bibliographers
6. keeping bibliographers informed of developments that affect their work
7. helping bibliographers to solve collection development problems
8. encouraging the professional development of bibliographers
9. evaluating the performance of bibliographers
10. maintaining appropriate contact with vendors
11. representing the library in cooperative collection development or preservation planning

4.2.1.1. Communication mechanisms used by the Collection Development Officer

Formal and informal communication mechanisms that the Collection Development Officer will routinely employ should be specified, along with their purposes as appropriate.

Examples of formal communications are written memoranda, articles, and notices in library publications, ad hoc discussions scheduled with one or more bibliographers on particular topics, regular meetings with specified groups.

4.2.1.2. A position description for the Collection Development Officer may be included in the manual.

4.2.2. Bibliographer obligations and responsibilities relating to the administration of the collection development and management program

The following are examples only and may vary considerably from one library to another:

1. annually analyzing expenditures for subject from all sources
2. preparing an annual budget request for submission to the Collection Development Officer
3. reporting to the Collection Development Officer on program information (amplified in 4.3.2 of this guide), the results of collection evaluations, and publishing trends
4. maintaining effective working relationship with the Collection Development Officer
5. maintaining effective working relationships with other bibliographers, emphasizing good communication on matters of mutual interest
6. informing the responsible person or body (such as the Collection Development Committee) of collection policy decisions negotiated with other bibliographers
7. supervising other bibliographers
8. supervising support staff

4.2.2.1. Types of communication, formal and informal, that the bibliographer is responsible for initiating should be specified; and appropriate communication mechanisms should be listed.

Examples of information that the bibliographer should convey to the Collection Development Officer throughout the year are:

1. user complaints and compliments about the collection
2. special funding needs
3. special preservation needs
4. new publishing and pricing trends in the field
5. significant plans for collection evaluation
6. areas requiring weeding
7. outstanding publications, antiquarian catalogs, auctions, etc.
8. recommendations, suggestions, requests
9. availability of large monetary gifts
10. large gifts of materials expected or received
11. subject areas in which coordinated acquisitions or cooperative preservation should be pursued
12. special funding available through Federal and state grants

4.2.2.2. Periodic written reports that may be required of bibliographers are amplified in 4.3.

4.3. Tools for collection development planning and decision making

Information transmitted by bibliographers to the Collection Development Officer in required reports is a valuable tool for planning and decision making. The kinds of written reports needed by the Collection Development Officer will vary according to the local environment.

The following are examples of written reports that either separately or in combination might be required of bibliographers on an annual basis:

4.3.1. The annual report

1. State the purpose(s) of the report, e.g., for the bibliographer to convey information on the year's collection development and management activities, to provide information relevant to fund allocation, to provide a basis for the individual bibliographer's performance evaluation.
2. Specify the scope of the report, including a statement on points for inclusion, both required and optional (one possible framework is reporting what has been done to meet old goals and objectives and establish new ones).

4.3.2. Program information

The bibliographer needs to record and present to the Collection Development Officer program data appropriate to collection development and management decision making. The presentation of the information can be organized through the use of a form. Program information may be provided as part of the annual budget process or in a separate operation.

4.3.2.1. Program data for academic libraries could include information on undergraduate and graduate enrollments; full-time equivalent faculty; plans for new courses, new programs, and new faculty; and use data.

4.3.2.2. Program data for public libraries might describe both the user constituency and use patterns.

Include here specific information on library users not already covered by the more general mission and goals statements or other documents. Such information might include population characteristics such as age, educational level attained, occupation, and ethnic background; a profile of purposes for which the collections are used; or other useful data on constituencies relevant to reading habits and collection development.

4.3.2.3. Program data for special libraries could include planned research projects, product development, or other activities in particular specialties; changes in emphasis by the parent institution, long- and short-range plans for the local organization; use data.

4.3.2.4. Program data for public school libraries might include statistics on special education collections, professional collections for faculty curriculum development, and particular areas of the general collections such as media or subjects targeted for curriculum revision.

4.3.3. Explanation of fund allocation process and guidelines for budget request statement

Describe the fund allocation process and the point at which the budget request statement is introduced into that process, with schedules shown in the calendar of events. Explain budget criteria, including possibly the use of program information, the results of collection evaluations as related to program needs, the mix of type of materials acquired in the field (e.g., periodicals, monographs, technical reports, software, videocassettes) together with their costs per unit, the amount of current production in the field, or the application of formulae.

An analysis of the previous year's expenditures for the subject, by type, from all sources may also be made a part of this document.

4.4. Recruiting bibliographers

4.4.1. Qualifications: education and experience

4.4.2. Anticipated applicant pool

The library's policy for filling bibliographer responsibilities, whether through specific external recruiting or through a part-time or full-time reassignment of someone already on the staff, should be stated. Describe the method for establishing a pool when bibliographer responsibilities are to be filled through reassignment.

4.4.3. Examples of specific bibliographer job descriptions may be included here. More general functions common to all bibliographers participating in the collection development and management program are enumerated in 5.3.

4.4.4. The role of the Collection Development Officer in the recruiting process should be described.

4.5. Orientation and training

The major features of the orientation/training program, which is developed and maintained by the Collection Development Officer or that person's designate, should be described in the manual, and other relevant documentation should be included. Note that for school librarians the terms *workshops* and *continuing education* might typically be applied to the orientation or training process. The extent of the incorporation of orientation for collection development into the general orientation program will depend on the size of the library and other local factors.

4.5.1. Some possible features of an orientation or training program are:

1. orientation sessions in other functional areas of collection development and management (e.g., preservation)
2. orientation sessions in functional areas that are related to collection development and management but are not organizational components of the program
3. hands-on experience in the functional areas noted above, including experience with media hardware

4. a protégé-mentor relationship with an experienced bibliographer for an extended period of time
   5. participant evaluation of the program

4.5.2. Other orientation and training documentation for inclusion

   1. Explain the specific use made of this manual in the orientation and training process.
   2. Detail the bibliographer's interaction with the Collection Development Officer during and at the end of the process.
   3. Include an orientation checklist to detail the points to be covered in each activity under each phase of the program.

4.6. Performance evaluation and goal setting

A statement describing procedures and criteria for evaluation of bibliographers with an indication of the frequency should be included in this section, with schedules shown in the calendar of events. Possibly the procedures will involve a written annual report, as noted in 4.3.1. This section of the manual should provide information useful to the bibliographer in establishing goals, setting deadlines, and documenting achievement as a basis for performance evaluation.

4.7. Professional development opportunities

List here the opportunities for professional development offered by the library or its parent agency, for example: work time to attend relevant lectures, classes, workshops, and seminars in the library or in the parent institution; paid travel and registration fees for professional conferences and similar meetings, where benefit to the parent institution may be demonstrated; released time for research assignments. Note that professional and intellectual development, from the perspective of the individual bibliographer, is addressed in 5.2 of these guidelines.

4.8. Calendar of events

Place in the manual a schedule of significant collection development dates throughout the year to permit appropriate planning and to reduce time conflicts with other programmatic areas. Scheduled events may include the institutional budgetary cycle, the internal budget request deadline, the collection development annual report deadline, book order deadlines, dates of regular, scheduled meetings related to collection development, and other information that will assist the bibliographer in planning the year's work. Academic and school libraries may also include relevant dates from the academic calendar; public libraries may include dates for program events, such as film festivals, children's reading programs, meetings of adult interest groups; and special librarians may wish to note such events as project deadlines and other organizational programs.

5. The bibliographer or subject specialist

5.1. Introduction

This section should define the local library's general conception of the bibliographer's role, responsibilities, and authority, indicating overall level and type of institutional expectations. These will vary considerably from one library to another, depending on administrative structures and styles as well as on the goals of the collection development program. Because they directly determine the kind of judgment and initiative properly exercised by bibliographers, such institutional expectations ought to be stated as explicitly as possible.

5.2. Intellectual and professional development

The bibliographer's personal obligation to achieve or expand competence and demonstrate continuing growth, not only in areas of subject specialization but also in the literature of collection management and development, should be stated. While the library's formal criteria for performance evaluation in this area are specified under 4.6 and the level of library support offered for professional development is detailed in 4.7, the particular value of these activities for bibliographers and the importance attached to them, as realized through national and regional service, scholarly publications, continuing education and related activities, also deserves explanation.

5.3. Job duties or responsibilities

Emphasis here is on the functions common to all staff participating in the library's collection development and management program. Excluded are administrative obligations otherwise covered under 4.2.2.

5.3.1. Selection of materials

Subsections here list the various activities that typically comprise the selection process. Individual libraries may wish to present these in priority order to reflect local circumstances. Techniques for implementing these activities can also be usefully specified at this point.

5.3.1.1. The collection development policy

The bibliographer's role in formulating, monitoring, and revising those portions of the library's collection development policy appropriate to specific subject and/or format assignments ought to be stated fully. Among the elements of potential local relevance the following might be noted:

1. description of established means for monitoring policy effectiveness and indication of the expected frequency of its routine review by bibliographers.
2. specification of the types of changes that mandate policy review (e.g., changing patterns of research, altered curricula, shifts in the demography of clientele). Suggested techniques for gathering this infor-

mation are included in Liaison with clientele (5.3.2) and Collection evaluation (5.3.4).
3. explanation of administrative channels and procedures for revising and approving changes in the collection policy

5.3.1.2. Monographs selection: typical activities should be identified and listed.

Examples are:
1. identification, use, and periodic revision of working lists of selection tools
2. managing and monitoring approval and blanket order plans, including establishing, evaluating and revising profiles, reviewing receipts for return or addition to the collection
3. title-by-title decisions for purchase of both current and retrospective items that are outside the coverage of gathering plans
4. title-by-title decisions for non-purchase items, such as gifts, exchange, and depository materials
5. generation of appropriate desiderata files and out-of-print search lists for areas of the collection determined to need strengthening
6. identification of sources for the acquisition of difficult to locate materials, both current and out-of-print materials

5.3.1.3. Serials selection

Parallel to 5.3.1.2, this section covers the bibliographer's serials-related selection activities, among which the following are typical:
1. establishing core lists of serials that are consistent with the local collection development policy and appropriate for acquisition by subscription or continuation order
2. developing procedures for identifying and evaluating new serial titles for acquisition on a continuation or subscription basis
3. ascertaining individual titles or classes of serials in need of backruns
4. establishing lists of monographic series not acquired by continuation order but which merit particular scrutiny for title-by-title selection

5.3.1.4. Media and microforms selection

Many of the activities mentioned under Monographs selection and Serials selection will also be relevant to the selection of media and microforms. In addition, bibliographers selecting these formats are usually expected to:
1. determine compatibility of media selections with existing equipment
2. maintain awareness of new formats and familiarity with their equipment requirements, recommending new kinds of equipment as desirable

5.3.1.5. Preservation and the initial selection decision

The manual needs to explain the local importance of preservation in the initial selection decision. Examples of such preservation concerns are:
1. the current physical condition of the material selected
2. expected durability of the material selected
3. cost of preservation upon receipt, as an addition to purchase price
4. durability and costs of alternate formats
5. adequacy of equipment and storage for media and microform selection

5.3.1.6. Knowledge of the world of publishing as it relates to selection responsibilities should be addressed.

Quality and scope of publishers; trends and statistics on the production, price, and marketing of information resources; and copyright and license agreements are areas of possible interest.

5.3.1.7. Vendor and bookseller relations

Bibliographers may have responsibility for maintaining relations with vendors and booksellers, ranging from knowing the existence of specialized dealers (particularly for locating retrospective materials), through contacting booksellers at conferences, to choosing and evaluating vendors for all their orders. The manual explains local requirements.

5.3.1.8. Buying trips

Depending on selection responsibilities and local circumstances, bibliographers may employ buying trips as a selection and acquisition strategy. Trips may be limited, for example, to one specialized out-of-town bookstore or annual book fair, or they may be so extensive as to cover several foreign countries.

5.3.2. Liaison with clientele

Regular communication with the library's clientele provides information essential to routine collection development operations as well as to longer range policy and planning. The bibliographer's responsibilities for establishing contacts, gathering appropriate patron opinions and user community data, and integrating these into the decision-making process should be fully explained. Channels of communication thereby established are also a means for interpreting the library's collections and its collecting program to patrons and may additionally offer opportunities for user education. For this public service aspect of liaison, see 5.3.6.

Collections-related areas that might be treated in the manual, depending on local circumstances, are:
1. mechanisms for communication, both formal channels (e.g., through academic chairpersons, library representatives, project managers,

chairpersons of Friends or citizens' interest groups), and informal means of contact
2. types and purposes of information regularly sought (e.g., advice on special or large purchases, background data on program or research emphases in the academic or special library community, responses to programs in the public library setting, reactions to proposed revisions in policy, procedures, or services)
3. role of liaison in publicizing collection development goals and objectives
4. statement of extent to which liaison function extends to non-collection development and management concerns (e.g., patron questions related to processing)

5.3.3. Collection management

Maximizing the utility of materials acquired for a library's collection is a complex task that begins with initial receipt and continues indefinitely thereafter. Bibliographers ought to be involved in this managerial process at numerous points, and their responsibilities at each juncture should be detailed. Subsections below cover some characteristic collection management duties of bibliographers.

5.3.3.1. Preservation

Subject specialization typically enables bibliographers to make well informed decisions about the importance of both the intellectual content and the physical attributes of materials whose actual or prospective deterioration requires preservation attention.

The following are representative duties for bibliographers in this arena:

1. identifying individual items and categories of deteriorating library materials that require preservation. Condition surveys conducted on a subject or format basis can identify areas of the collection, such as German 19th-century theology, 16mm. films, or folios, that are in need of preservation.
2. identifying valuable library materials that according to local policy can be appropriately placed in a limited access location
3. applying local criteria for preservation selection and understanding the differences between these and those used for current selection
4. recommending preservation options appropriate for library resources that cannot be repaired, e.g., withdrawal, replacement (with exact copy, reprint, other edition, microform), no treatment, or conservation of the item as an artifact
5. setting priorities for conservation of artifactual materials
6. setting salvage priorities for incorporation into the library's disaster preparedness plan
7. helping to educate staff and users on preservation concerns, including proper handling of library materials

5.3.3.2. Monitoring collection use

Typically this activity helps the bibliographer to identify:

1. titles needed in additional copies, new editions, or new formats
2. lesser-used materials for withdrawal from the collection or removal to remote access storage
3. periodicals appropriate for converting backruns to microform instead of binding

5.3.3.3. Advising the library's technical processing unit

The bibliographer may be expected to advise on aspects of technical processing related to the area of subject expertise, for example:

1. processing priorities dictated by special research, curricular, and/or clientele concerns
2. cataloging and binding issues arising from intellectual content and/or anticipated patron approach to materials (e.g., whether analytics are needed when volumes of a monographic series are classified together)
3. acceptability of incomplete volumes of current periodicals

5.3.4. Collection evaluation

The individual bibliographer's role in assessing the library's collection will vary according to the occasion, scope, and design of particular evaluation projects. Sometimes the study is focused on a narrow segment of the total collection; the choice of method in these instances properly resides with the bibliographer. At other times evaluations prompted by broader institutional concerns can affect large portions of the collection, and methods may therefore be prescribed.

Information on preservation needs can be a useful byproduct of an evaluation project, though the primary objective may be quite different.

5.3.4.1. Purposes for evaluation

Reasons typically motivating evaluations of the local library's collection should be noted, with an indication of the bibliographer's characteristic role in each circumstance. Some common occasions of evaluation include:

1. accreditation reports
2. new degree and program proposals
3. studies of the strength of the collection in selected subjects to verify effectiveness of collection development policy and/or to identify areas for retrospective development
4. initiation of a coordinated collection development plan

5.3.4.2. Methods for evaluation

To assure consistency and reliability of results, bibliographers should be cautioned to exercise particular care when selecting techniques for assessing the collection. The Resources and Technical Services Division guidelines, *Guide to the Evaluation of Library Collections* (currently in draft), inventory a variety of useful methods, indicating their advantages and disadvantages. The local choice of an assessment technique should consider the factors summarized in this document.

5.3.4.3. Results of collection evaluations

The manual should specify how the bibliographer is expected to communicate the results of evaluation activities and the format in which the information should be reported. When standard forms have been developed for this purpose, the forms should be appended to the manual.

5.3.5. Fund management

The individual bibliographer's responsibility for authorizing encumbrances will vary among libraries, as will the specific limitations and exceptions placed on it. The exact scope of this responsibility should be described fully since it largely determines the bibliographer's range of duties in the area of fund management. Typical duties that may be locally relevant follow.

5.3.5.1. Monitoring expenditures to assure proper rate of encumbrance and expenditure during the fiscal year

The mechanisms for this process will depend on the local accounting system with its style and frequency of reporting financial data. The distinctive features of local accounting procedures as they affect the monitoring of acquisitions funds should be explained. Techniques for compensating for inadequate or delayed information should also be noted. Examples of expenditure reports and a glossary of special terminology may be usefully included in this section or appended as supporting documents.

5.3.5.2. Other fund management activities may include:

1. compiling and justifying regular budget requests (institutional procedures, criteria, and budgeting schedule are treated in 4.3.3)
2. analyzing on an annual basis the total expenditure of funds for area of responsibility from all sources
3. preparing and justifying requests for major purchases or other special funding
4. negotiating the cooperative funding of expensive items with other bibliographers and with other libraries
5. preparing proposals for alternative funding

5.3.6. Collection interpretation

Because of their combined collection development experience and subject expertise, bibliographers are often assigned collection interpretation duties. The amount and nature of this service will vary considerably among libraries. Representative of the range of activities in this area are the following:

1. providing direct user instruction, including tours, classroom presentations, and public lectures
2. providing general and specialized reference services
3. preparing exhibits and publications to highlight aspects of the library's collections
4. compiling user aids designed to introduce patrons to the bibliography of particular topics and the corresponding local resources

INDEX

Annual report, 12
Approval plan (definition), 2
    acquisitions strategy, 6

Bibliographer (definition), 2
    administrative obligations, 11-12
    goal setting, 15
    job duties, 16-22
    orientation, 14-15
Blanket order (definition), 2
    acquisitions strategy, 6
Budget process, 11, 12-14, 21
Buying trips, 18

Calendar of events, 15
Collection development (definition), 2
Collection development and management program (definition), 2
Collection development officer (definition), 2
    administrative obligations, 10-11
    communication mechanisms used by, 11
    position description, 11
    role in recruiting, 14
Collection development policy (definition), 2
    history and present status, 6
    bibliographer's role in, 16-17
Collection evaluation, 20-21
Collection interpretation, 21-22
Collection management (definition), 3
    bibliographer's responsibility for, 19-20
Collection use, 20
Committee structure, 10
Communication
    by collection development officer, 11
    by bibliographer, 12
    annual report, 13
    liaison with clientele, 18-19
    program information, 13
    results of collection evaluation, 21
Conservation (definition), 3
Cooperative activities, 9
    cooperative funding, 21
    coordinated collection development, 9
    collection evaluation, 20
Core list (definition), 3
    in serials selection, 17

Depository arrangement (definition), 3
    acquisitions strategy, 6
Directory of bibliographers, 10
Disaster preparedness plan (definition), 3
    other publications, 6
    salvage priorities, 19
Disposition policy (definition), 3
    other publications, 6

Exchange agreement (definition), 3
Expenditures, monitoring, 21

Fund allocation (definition), 3
    explanation of process, 13-14
Fund management, 21

Gathering plan (definition), 3
    acquisitions strategy, 6
Goal setting, 15
Guides and guidelines, 8-9

Liaison with clientele, 18-19
Library functions, related, 7

Media (definition), 4
    selection, 17

23

Mission and goals statement, 5

National standards, 8-9

Organization charts, 10
Orientation, 14-15

Performance evaluation, 15
Policies, local, 6-7
Preservation (definition), 4
    and the initial selection decision, 17-18
    as part of collection management, 19
Professional development, 16
Program information, 13
Publications and policies
    local, 6-7
    national, 8-9
Publishers and publishing, 18

Recruiting, 14
Remote storage, 20

Selection of materials, general approach, 6
    media and microforms, 17
    monographs, 17
    preservation and initial selection, 17-18
    serials, 17
Standards, national, 8
Standing order (definition), 4
    acquisitions strategy, 6
Subscription (definition), 4
    serials selection, 17
Support staff, 10
    collection development officer and, 11
    supervision by bibliographer, 12

Technical processing advice, 20
Training for bibliographers, 14-15

User instruction, 22

Vendor relations, 18